CHRISTIAN HOME,

AS IT IS IN THE

Sphere of Nature and the Church.

BY

REV. SAMUEL PHILIPS, A. M.,

PASTOR OF THE FIRST GERMAN REFORMED CHURCH, CHAMBERSBURG, PA.

"Sweet is the smile of Home! the mutual look
When hearts are of each other sure;
Sweet all the joys that crowd the household nook,
The haunt of all affections pure."

KEBLE.

SPRINGFIELD, MASS.:
PUBLISHED BY G. & F. BILL.
1859.

These instructions on courtship and inheritance have been extracted from this book *"The Christian Home"* By Rev. Samuel Philips in 1859.

Courtship

By: Rev. Samuel Philips

MERCHANT ADVENTURERS
WAKE FOREST, NORTH CAROLINA

Second Printing: September 2008

Merchant Adventurers, Inc.
3721 Quarry Rd Wake Forest North Carolina 27587
www.scottbrownonline.com

ISBN-10: 0-9820567-1-0
ISBN-13: 978-0-9820567-1-4

Book Design By David Edward Brown

Printed in the United States of America

Table of Contents

Thoughts on "Courtship"

By Scott Brown

Preparing your children to be married and then guiding them through the selection process can be like walking through a mine field. People may use similar language to explain how they want to go about "courting" or "betrothal' or "dating", but the definitions of these terms may be as diverse and personal as one's DNA. People often use a confusing array of terminology to explain how they want to engage in this process and it often leads to misunderstanding.

These problems are inflamed because we often use terminology that is not found in scripture and is subject to private interpretation. This just means that we ought to be careful to define terms so others understand what we mean by what we say. For example, if we use words like "courtship" and "dating" which do not appear in scripture, we ought to make sure we understand what biblical principles we are loading into these words.

Here are some of the conclusions I have come to on the matter of the pre-marital relationship.

First, scripture presents sufficient principles.

I believe that scripture presents patterns that are workable and applicable, but I don't believe that scripture provides a single formula for governing the process. There are authoritative commands and principles that govern sexuality (Galatians 5:13-26), community (Ephesians 4:1-16), the nature of marriage (Ephesians 5:22-33), and the creation order relationships (Ephesians 6:1-4). These are beacons of light shining on our paths.

At the same time, I am not comfortable presenting airtight cookie cutter formulas to guide every part of the courtship process. Scripture seems to present a diversity of applications, for there are simply no courtship/marriage stories which are exactly alike. I believe this means that God has designed flexibility in the process and He expects us to walk in a manner worthy of the Lord, using scripture to guide our steps.

Second, the current dating system is unbiblical and destructive.

The patterns of dating and it's underlying principles are worldly, bankrupt and fraught with faith diluting and marriage destroying, evangelism hampering elements (Romans 1:1-2). Consider these five marks of dating in our day. It features random engagements instead of strategic engagements; multiple engagements instead of carefully considered engagements; individualistic inclinations and passions instead of kingdom conscious thinking; romantic methodology instead of principled methodology; immoral relationships instead of proactively pure relationships.

The process of getting and staying married is severely malfunctioning in our land. With the divorce rate in the church statistically indistinguishable from the unbelieving world, it would not be considered hyperbole to say that today's marriages in the churches are a moral disaster. As we have slowly adopted the ways of the world in nearly every area of life in order to maintain our respectability, at the same time, we have lost our ability to properly join our children in marriage. Our children have been left with unworkable methods in a broken godless system.

This is why I hope these culturally acceptable practices would be abandoned by the church and replaced with more rational and intentionally biblical approaches.

Third, I hold to five principles for handling the pre-marital relationship.

First, the couple must honor parental authority and responsibility. Scripture makes fathers the heads of their sons and daughters, (Numbers 30, Ephesians 6:1-4), which is why I do not believe that it is appropriate for suitors to woo my daughters without my permission. Suitors are not allowed to relate with my daughters in a way that would attempt to win them until I am convinced of the wisdom of moving forward. Because of the structural headship of our household, it is appropriate for the couple to cheerfully place themselves under my timelines and requirements. Why would I have these constraints? One reason is that I want to avoid premature, vain twitterpations and multiple mini divorces before my children are married.

Second, wise counselors who know the couple must be consulted and there should be a general affirmation of the marriage (Genesis 24, Proverbs 15:22).

Third, a process of interviewing and screening is necessary to establish equal yoking and compatible values (2 Corinthians 6:14).

Fourth, the couple should have a genuine tender love for one another and passion for the marriage, and not be forced into it (Genesis 24:67).

Fifth, purity must be maintained according to biblical definitions and protections should be in place to assist in moral success(Colossians 3:5).

I pray that we in the church will not follow the ways of the gentiles in our pre-marital practices, but that we will glorify God with sweet courtships, betrothals and marriages, honoring the Word of God and dedicated to Christ and His wonderful kingdom.

About the Book

The following thoughts on preparation for marriage and inheritance come from the Rev. Samuel Philips, in a book he published in 1859, entitled, "*The Christian Home, as it is in the Sphere of the Nature and the Church.*" This book is full of practical wisdom for home and church life. This section of the book on matchmaking has been extracted from the whole in order to highlight the subject matter.

I felt this should be reprinted because Mr. Philips has helpful insights into some of the problems of helping our children get married. There are many difficulties that parents and children encounter during this process and there is really not much written on the subject. I thought it would be helpful to bring the thinking of someone outside of our cultural milieu to help us consider the issues.

Some may read what he has written and feel that he has not said enough or answered all the questions that one might have. It is true that Mr. Philips does not answer every question, nor does he provide answers for every situation, but he does address many important issues that I trust will be helpful.

Mr. Philips' thinking will cause us to make progress for strategic, thoughtful, God conscious marriages. What is needed in the church today are principled thoughtful marriages for the glory of God.

Chapter One

The House Parlor

Preparing your home for considering marriage partners

The Christian home includes the parlor. This department we must give but a brief and passing notice. Yet it is as important and responsible as the nursery. In it we have a view of the relations of home to society beyond it. The parlor is set apart for social communion with the world. Much of momentous interest is involved in this relation. The choice of companions, the forming of attachments and matrimonial alliances, the establishment of social position and influence in life beyond the family. These are all involved in the home-parlor.

Why hold this period of time as sacred?

If we would, therefore, escape the shackles and contamination of corrupt society, we must hold the parlor sacred and give to it the air and bearing of at least a moral aristocracy. Home is the first form of society. The law of love rules and reigns there. It is enthroned in the heart, and casts light around our existence. In that society we live above the trammels of artificial life. In its parlor the members merge with society beyond its sacred precincts. Hence it is the most beautiful room, the best furniture is there; smiles adorn it. Friends meet there; fashion meets there in her silks and jewels, with her circumstance and custom, her sympathies, antipathies and many kinds of conversation; form and profession reign there; flatteries and hypocrisies intrude themselves there; pledges are given there; attachments and vows are made there; the mind and heart are impressed and molded there; the cobweb lines of etiquette are drawn there; a panorama of social fascinations pass before the youthful eye there. These make the parlor the most dangerous department of home. There the young receive their first introduction to society; there they see the world in all the brilliancy of outward life, in the pomp and pageantry of a vanity fair. All seems to them as a fairy dream, as a brilliant romance; their hearts are allured by these outward attractions; their imaginations are fed upon the unreal, and they learn to judge character by the external trappings in which its reality is concealed. They estimate worth by the beauty of the face and form, by the cost of dress and the movements of the body. They form their notions of happiness from fashion, fortune and position. They become enslaved to lovesick novels and fashionable amusements. There, too, they make choice of companions; there they form matrimonial alliances; there their hearts are developed, their minds trained for social life, their affections directed, and influence brought to bear upon them, which will determine their well being or their woe.

Guarding this time of life

If this is the influence of the home-parlor, should it not be held sacred, and made to correspond in all the uses for which it is set apart, with the spirit and character of a Christian family; and should not its doors be effectually guarded against the intrusion of spurious and demoralizing elements of society? Parents should teach their children all about the character, interests and deceptions of parlor-life. They should undeceive them in their natural proneness to judge people from the standpoint of character assumed in the parlor. They see the lamb there, but not the lion; the smile but not the frown; the affability of manner, but not the tyranny of spirit. They hear the language of flattery, but not the tongue of slander. They see no weak points, detect no evil temper and bad habits. There is an artificial screen behind which all that is revolting and dangerous is concealed. Who would venture to judge a person by his mechanical movements in the parlor? Many are there the very opposite to what they are elsewhere.

"Abroad too kind, at home 'tis steadfast hate, and one eternal tempest of debate. What foul eruptions from a look most meek! What thunders bursting from a dimpled cheek! Such dead devotion, such zeal for crimes, such licensed ill, such masquerading times, such venal faiths, such misapplied applause, such flattered guilt, and such inverted laws!"

A dangerous season

One of the most dangerous periods of life is when we leave the nursery and school, and enter the parlor. With what solicitude, therefore, should Christian parents guard their parlors from social corruption. They should prepare their children for society, not only by teaching them its manners and customs, how to act in company, how to grace a party, and move with refined ease among companions there, but also by teaching them the dangers and corruptions which lurk in their midst and follow in the train of rustling silks and fashionable drama. They should never permit their parlor to become the scene of fashionable tyranny. The Christian parlor can be no depot for fashion. It should be sacred to God and to the church. It should be a true exponent of the social elements of Christianity. It should not be a hermitage, a state of seclusion from the world; but should conform to fashion yet so far only as the laws of a sanctified taste and refinement will admit.

These laws exclude all compromise and amalgamation with the ungodly spirit and customs of the world. Allegiance to the higher and better law of God will keep us from submission to the laws of a depraved taste and carnal desire. We must keep ourselves unspotted from the world. Whenever we submit with scrupulous exactness to the laws of fashion; whenever we yield a servile complaisance to its forms and ceremonies, wink at its extremes and immoralities and absurd expenditures, seek its flatteries and indulge in its whims and caprices, by throwing open our parlors as the theatre of their plot, and introducing our children to their actors and master-spirits, we prostitute our homes, our religion and those whom God has given us to train up for Himself, to interests and pleasures the most unworthy of the Christian name and character.

Attractions away from home can destroy the enjoyment of one another

There is much danger now of the Christian home becoming in this way slavishly bound to the influence and attractions of society beyond the pale of the church, until all relish for home-enjoyment is lost, and its members no longer seek and enjoy each other's association. They drain the cup of voluptuous pleasure to its dregs, and flee from home as dull. The husband leaves his wife, and seeks his company in fashionable saloons, at the card table or in halls of revelry. The wife leaves the society of her children, and in company with a bosom companion, seeks to throw off the tedium of home, at masquerade meetings, at the theater or in the ball-room, where

"Vice, once by modest nature chained, and legal ties, expatiates unrestrained; without thin decency held up to view, naked she stalks o'er law and gospel too!"

Children often go their own way

The children follow their example; become disgusted with each other's company, and sacrifice their time and talents to a thousand little trifles and absurdities. Taste becomes depraved, and loses all relish for national enjoyment. The heart teems with idle fancies and vain imaginations. Sentimentalism takes the place of religion; filthy literature and fashionable cards shove the Family Bible in some obscure nook of their parlor and their hearts. The hours devoted to family prayer are now spent in a giddy whirl of amusement and intoxicating pleasure, in the study of the latest fashions and of the newly-published love adventures of some nabob in the world of refined scoundrelism. The parental solicitude, once directed to the eternal welfare of the child, is now expended in match-making and setting out in the world.

Unfit influences creep in during this season

Thus does the Christian home often become adulterated with the world by its indiscriminate association with unfit social elements. That portion of society whose master-spirits are love-stricken poets, languishing girls, amorous grandmothers, and sap-headed fiction writers, is certainly unfit for a place in the parlor of the Christian family. We should not permit the principles of common-sense decorum to give place to the lawless vagaries of fancy and the hollow-hearted forms of artificial life. Under the gaudy drapery of smiles and flounces, of rustling silks and blandishments, there are hearts as brutish and stultified, and heads as brainless and incapable of gentle and moral emotion, and characters as selfish and ungenerous, as were ever concealed beneath the rags of poverty, or the uncouth manners and rough garb of the incarcerated villain!

Unspotted home life must be maintained during this time.

It is, therefore, beneath the dignity of the Christian to permit his home to become in any way a prey to immoral and irreligious associations and influences. Like the personal character of the Christian, it should be kept unspotted from the world; and no spirit, no customs, no companions, opposed to religion, should be permitted to enter its sacred limits. Heedless of this important requisition, parents may soon see their children depart from the ways in which they were trained in the nursery, and at last become a curse to them, and bring down their gray hairs with sorrow to the grave.

Beware of inadequate guardianship during this time

Here is indeed the great fault of many Christian parents in the present day. They do not exert that guardian care they should over the social relations and interests of their children. They are too unscrupulous in their introduction to the world, and leave them in ignorance of its snares and deceptions. What results can they look for if they permit their parlor tables to become burdened with French novels, and their children to mingle in company whose influence is the most detrimental to the interests of pure and undefiled religion? Can they reflect upon their daughters for forming improper attachments and alliances? Can they wonder if their sons become desperadoes, and ridicule the religion of their parents? No! They permitted them to dally with the fangs of a viper which found a ready admittance into their parlor; and upon them, therefore, will rest the responsibility, yea the deep and eternal curse!

Parents will be held responsible

Woe unto you, thou unfaithful parent; the voice of your children's blood shall send up from the hallowed ground of home, one loud and penetrating cry to God for vengeance; and thou shalt be "beaten with many stripes." It will not only cry out against you, but cling to you!

Guard this time from corrupting companions

Guard your parlor, therefore, from the corrupting influence of all immoral associations. Be not carried away by the pomp and glare of refined and decorated wickedness. Let not the ornaments and magnificence of mere outward life divert your attention from those hidden principles which prompt to action. In the choice of companions for your children in the parlor, look to the ornaments of the heart rather than to those of the body. Be not allured by the parade of circumstance and position in life. Be not carried away by that which may intoxicate for a moment, and then leave the heart in more wretchedness than before. Ever remember that the future condition of your children, their domestic character and happiness, will depend upon the kind of company you admit in your parlor. This leads us to the consideration of the part Christian parents should take in the marriage of their children. This we shall investigate in our next chapter under the head of "Match-making."

Chapter Two

Match Making

Parental involvement in the marriage choices of their children

"Youth longs for a kindred spirit, and yet yearns for a heart that can commune with his own. Take heed that what charms you is real, not springs of your own imagination; and suffer not trifles to win your love for a wife is yours unto death!"

The bridal hour

One of the most affecting scenes of home-life is that of the bridal hour! Though in one sense it is a scene of joy and festivity; yet in another, it is one of deep sadness. When all is adorned with flowers and smiles, and the parlor becomes the theater of conviviality and parade, even then hearts are oppressed with sorrow at the thought of that separation which is soon to take place.

It is a time of crisis

The bridal is a home-crisis. It is the breaking up of home-ties and communion, a separation from home scenes, a lopping off from the parent vine, an engrafting into a strange vine, and alas! too often, into a degenerate vine. As the youthful bride stands beside her affianced husband, to be wedded to him for life, and reflects that the short ceremonial of that occasion will tear her forever from the loved objects and scenes of her childhood home. What tears of bitter sorrow adorn the bridal cheek, and what pungent feelings are awakened by her last farewell !

A brides farewell

"I leave you, sister! We have played through many a joyous hour, where the silvery gleam of the olive shade hung dim o'er fount and bower."

"Yes! I leave you, sister, with all that we have enjoyed together; I leave you in the memory of our childhood haunts and song and prayer. We cannot be as we have been. I leave you now, and all that has bound us together as one; and hereafter memory alone can hail you, and will do so with her burning tear; therefore, kind sister, let me weep!"

"I leave you, father! Eve's bright moon, must now light other feet, with the gathered grapes, and the lyre in tune, your homeward steps to greet."

"Yes, I leave you, father! I receive your last blessing; no longer shall your protecting hand guide me; no longer shall your smile be music to my ear. I leave you, oh, therefore, let me weep!"

"Mother! I leave you! On your breast, pouring out joy and woe; I have found that holy place of rest still changeless yet I go!"

"Yes, I go from you, mother! Though you have watched over me in helpless infancy with all a mother's love and care, and lulled me with your rain; and though earth may not afford me a love like yours; yet I go! Oh, therefore, sweet mother, let me weep!"

"Oh, friends regretted, scenes forever dear remembrance hails you with her burning tear; drooping she bends o'er pensive fancy's urn, to trace the hours which ne'er can return."

How involved should parents be in the marriage choice?

If momentous interests are involved in marriage, then, we think that parents should take an important part in the matrimonial alliances of their children. When they grow up, they naturally seek a companion for life. The making choice of that companion is a crisis in their history, and will determine their future interest and happiness. If separation from home is a great sacrifice then, we should look well to the grounds of our justification in making that sacrifice.

We propose, under the head of "match-making" to consider the part which parents should take in the marriage of their children; and also the false and true standards of judgment both for parents and their children, in making the marriage choice and alliance.

Children need superior wisdom

Have parents a right to take any part in the marriage choice and alliance of their children? Have they a right to interfere in any respect with the marriage of their children? That they do possess such a right, and are justified in the exercise of it within just and reasonable limits, is, we think, undisputed by anyone acquainted with the Word of God. It is one of the cardinal prerogatives and duties of the Christian parent. His relation to his children invests him with it. The age and inexperience of the child, on the one hand; and the seductions of the world, on the other, imply it. Children need counsel and admonition; and this is a needs-be for the interposition of the parent's superior wisdom and greater experience.

The example of Abraham

This right is plainly exemplified in sacred history. Abraham interfered in Isaac's selection of a companion. Isaac and Rebecca aided in the choice of a wife for Jacob. And indeed throughout the patriarchal age, you find this right recognized and practiced. It was also acknowledged and exercised in all the subsequent ages of Judaism, in the age of primitive Christianity, and even down to the present time, in every true Christian household. The right still exists, and receives the sanction of the church. The great dereliction of parents now is, that they do not exercise it; and of children, that they do not recognize it. "A wise son hears his father's instructions." "The eye that mocks at his father, and despises to obey his mother, the ravens of the valley shall pluck it out, and the young eagles shall eat it."

What now is the extent, and what are the duties of that right to interfere? This is a difficult question, and can receive but an imperfect answer. In infancy the authority of the parent is exercised without any reference to the will of the child, because reason is not yet developed. But when he reaches the age of personal accountability, the control of the parent is exercised on more liberal principles; and when, by age, he becomes a responsible citizen, the legal authority of the parent ceases. Still he possesses moral authority, and has a right to exert a restraining influence over the child. This does not, of course, involve a right to compel him to yield to the parent's arbitrary will. He can exert but a moral control over him; and it is the child's duty to yield to this, so long as it is consistent with scripture and the maxims of sound reason and conscience. He should consult his parents, receive them into his confidence, and give priority to their judgment and counsels.

Preventing a bad marriage

Parents have the right to use coercive measures to prevent an imprudent marriage by their children before they have arrived at age; for until they are of age they are both legally and morally under the authority and government of their parents, who are responsible for them. Hence the child should recognize and submit to their authority. But this right to the use of coercive measures extends only to the prevention of unhappy marriages, not to the forming of what the parents may regard as happy alliances, against the will of the child. No parent has the right to compel a child under age to marry, because the marriage alliance implies the age and free choice of the child.

The importance of persuasive, not coercive authority

But when the child reaches legal maturity, the coercive authority of the parent ceases. His interposition then should not involve coercive, but persuasive measures. Then a mere mechanical prevention of an unhappy marriage would have no good moral effect, but would be productive of great evil, inasmuch as it not only involves parental despotism, but the restriction of a manifest and conceded right of the child. It would destroy the sense of personal dignity and responsibility.

Avoid unreasonable extremes

Persuasive measures will then accomplish more than all the efforts of the parent to prevent an unhappy union, by threats of disinheritance and expulsion from home. In this way parents often extend their interference to most unreasonable extremes, and to the great detriment of the interests and happiness of their children; while at the same time they often bring disgrace and misery upon their own heads and home. They set themselves up as the choosers of companions for their children, presuming that they should passively submit to their selection whatever it may be. This is taking away the free moral agency of the child, making no account of his taste, judgment, or affections; and forming between him and the object thus chosen a mere outward union, with no inward affinity.

Acknowledge sinister motives

In such cases it most generally happens that parents are prompted by sinister motives and a false pride, as that of wealth, honor, and social position. They do not consult the law of suitability, but that of availability. They think that wealth and family distinction will compensate for the absence of all moral and amiable qualities, that if outward circumstances are favorable, there need not be inward adaptation of character. Hence they will dictate to their children, make their marriage alliance a mere business matter, and demand implicit obedience on the penalty of expulsion from the parental home, and disinheritance forever. They are thus willing to prostitute the domestic peace and happiness of their offspring to the gratification of their own sordid and inordinate lust for gain and empty distinction.

Perceive unfeeling despotism

Who does not perceive and acknowledge the evil of such a course? It involves unfeeling despotism on the one hand, and a servile obedience on the other. The affections are abused; the idea and sacredness of marriage are left out of view; the conditions of domestic felicity are not met. All is supremely selfish; the power exercised is arbitrary; the submission is slavish and demoralizing; the obedience involuntary and degrading; and the result of it all is, an outrage against nature, against marriage, and against God.

Engage in affectionate persuasion

On the other hand, the interference of the parent should be persuasive, and the obedience of the child, voluntary. The parent should reason with and counsel the child; and seek by mild and affectionate means to secure obedience to his advice. And if the child then persist in his own course, the parent, we think, has discharged his duty, and the responsibility will rest upon the child. He should not expel and disinherit him, and thus add the hard-heartedness of the parent to the folly and perversity of the child. He should love him still, and seek by parental tenderness to alleviate the sad fruits of filial recklessness. Parents should so train their children in the nursery and parlor, by instilling in them correct principles of judgment in the choice of a companion, as to secure them ever after from an imprudent choice. Here is the place to begin. Parents too often omit this duty, until alas, it is too late.

When one has no true affection

We have now seen that the parent has no right to destroy the domestic happiness of a child by uniting him forcibly in wedlock to one for whom he has no true affection. On the other hand, the child should pay due deference to the parent's moral suasion, and seek, if possible, to follow his counsels. "A child," says Paley, "who respects his parent's judgment, and is, as he ought to be, tender of their happiness, owes, at least, so much deference to their will, as to try fairly and faithfully, in one case, where time and absence will not cool an affection which they disapprove. After a sincere but ineffectual endeavor by the child, to accommodate his inclination to his parent's pleasure, he ought not to suffer in his parent's affections, or in his fortunes. The parent, when he has reasonable proof of this, should acquiesce; at all events, the child is then at liberty to provide for his own happiness."

Chapter Three

False Tests

False tests for selecting a companion for life

Before we turn to some of those biblical principles upon which parents and children should proceed in the marriage choice, we shall take a negative view of the subject, and mention some of those false principles and considerations which have in the present day gained a fearful ascendancy over the better judgment of many professed Christians.

Too much focus on outward appearance

In the matter of marriage, too many are influenced by the pomp and parade of the mere outward. The glitter of gold, the smile of beauty, and the array of titled distinction and circumstance act like a charm upon the feelings and sentiments of many well-meaning parents and children. But it is not all gold that glitters. We must not think that those are happy in their marriage union, because they are obsequious in their attention to each other, and live together in splendor, overloaded with fashionable congratulations. We cannot determine the character of a marriage from its pomp and pageantry. We rather determine the many unhappy matches from the false principles upon which the parties acted in making choice of each other. What are some of these? We answer.

1. The manner of relating to one another involves a false principle of procedure. These are either too long or too short, and paid in an improper spirit and manner. There is too much flirtation and romance connected with them. The religious element is not taken up and considered. They do not involve the true idea of preparation, but have an air of mere sentimentalism about them. The object in view is not fully seen. The most reprehensible motives and the most shocking thoughtlessness pervade them throughout. This manner of relating carries with it an air of trifling, a want of seriousness and frankness, which betrays the absence of all sense of responsibility, and of all proper views of the sacredness of marriage and of its momentous consequences both for time and for eternity.

2. The habit of match-making involves a false principle. This we see more fully among the higher classes of society. It is the work of designing and interested persons, who, for self-interest, intrude their unwelcome interposition. Its whole procedure implies that marriage is simply a legal matter, a piece of business policy, a domestic speculation. It strikes out the great law of mutual, moral love, and personal adaptation. It makes marriage artificial, and apprehends it as only a mechanical co-partnership of interest and life. It is sinister in spirit, and selfish in the end. Many are prompted from motives of novelty to make matches among their friends. All their schemes tend to wrest from the parties interested all true judgment and dispassionate consideration. They are deceived by base misrepresentation, allured by over-wrought pictures of conjugal felicity, so that when the marriage is consummated, they soon end and their golden dreams vanish away, and with them, their hopes and their happiness forever.

Personal matchmakers

But there are not only personal match-makers in the form of tyrannical fathers, sentimental mothers, amorous grandmothers, and obsequious friends; but also book match-makers, in the form of love-sick tales and poetry, containing Eugene Aram adventures and scrapes of languishing girls with titled admirers running off, calculated to heat the youthful imagination, distort the pictures of fancy, giving to marriage the air of a romantic adventure, and throwing over it a gaudy drapery, leading the young into a world of dreams and nonentities, where all is but a bubble of variegated colors and fantastic forms, which explodes before them as soon as it is touched by the finger of reality and experience.

Ballroom dance matchmaking

These are the most dangerous match-makers. Their sister companions in this evil are, the ballroom, the giddy dance and masquerade, the fashionable wine-cup, and the costly apparel. Let me affectionately exhort the members of the Christian home to keep all these at a distance. Touch not, taste not, handle not! They will poison the spirit and the affections, and encircle you with a viper's coil from which there is no hope of escape. Here parents have a right, and it is their duty, to interfere. They can do so effectually by not allowing such filthy match-making intruders to pass the threshold of their homes. What can you expect out of an unhappy marriage, if you permit your sons and daughters to spend their time in converse with love-sick tales and languishing swains? They will become love-sick, too, and long for marriage with one who is like the hero of their last read romance. Perhaps they will not think their matrimonial debut sufficiently flavored with romantic essence, unless they run off with some self-constituted count, or at least with their Papa's Irish groom!

3. There are false influences frequently brought to bear upon the children's choice of a companion for life.

Smitten by false love

The term smitten is here significant and deserves our serious consideration. It carries in its pregnant meaning the evidence of a spurious feeling, and a false foundation of love and union. Be it remembered that there must always be something to smite one. We may be smitten by a scoundrel, or by something unworthy of our affections. Empty titles and mustaches often smite the susceptible young. Sometimes the heart is smitten by a pretty face and form and sometimes by a rod of gold. The simple fact that we are smitten is not enough; we should know who or what it is that smites us. When we are drawn to each other, it should be by a true cord, and by an influence which binds and cements for life. The influence of mere outward beauty is a false one. Those who are smitten by it, and drawn thus into a monomial union by an interest which is but skin deep, and which may fade like the morning flower, are allured by a dazzling meteor, by a mere bubble, beautifully formed and colored, but empty within. It may dazzle the eye, but it blinds us to all its blemishes and inward infirmities. It is deceptive. Often beneath its gaudy veil there lies the viper, ready to poison all the sweets of home-life, and cause its victim to lament over his folly with bitter tears and heart burning remorse. How soon may beauty fade; and what then, if it was the only basis of your marriage choice? The union which rested upon it must then be at least morally dissolved; and that which once flitted like an impersonated charm before your admiring eye, now becomes an object of disgust and a source of misery.

Love for outward beauty

To fall in love, therefore, with mere outward beauty is to dandle with a doll, to fawn upon a picture, to rest your hopes upon a plaything, to pursue a phantom which, as soon as you embrace it may vanish into nothing. Look not to external beauty alone; but also to the ornaments of an inward spirit, of a noble mind, and an amiable and pious heart. "If," says the Rev. H. Harbaugh, "you will be foolish, follow the gilded butterfly of beauty, drive it a long chase; it will land you at last in some stagnant mud-pond of the highway."

Love at first sight

Neither is impulsive passion a true basis of marriage. This is falling in love at first sight, which often proves to be a very dangerous and degrading fall, a fall from the clouds to the clods, producing both humiliation and misery. It is indeed a fearful leap, a leap without judgment or forethought; and, therefore, a leap in the dark. It is too precipitate, and shows the infatuation of the victim. Falling in love is not always falling in the embrace of domestic felicity. Such leaping is an act of intoxication. The drunkard, falling in the mire, often thinks that he is embracing his best friend, whereas it is but descending to fellowship with the swine. It is blind love, which is no love, but passion without reason. It is crazy, fitful, stormy, raising the feelings up to boiling point, and bringing the affections under the influence of the high-pressure system. Consequently it is raving, frothy, of a mushroom growth, making mere bubbles, and completing its work in an evaporation of all that it operated upon, passing away like the morning cloud and the early dew.

True love is very different. It is substantial, reasonable, moral, acting according to law, temperate in all things, keeping the heart from extremes, permanent, and based upon principle. Passion, without love, may keep you in a state of pleasurable intoxication until the knot is tied, when you will soon get sober again, only to see however, your folly, and to contemplate the height from which you have fallen, and then, with the recklessness of sullen despair, to pass over into the opposite extreme of stoical indifference and misery. All emotions are transient, and hence no proper standard of judgment in the serious matter of a marriage choice. The heart, unguided by the head, is, in its emotions, like the flaming meteor that passes in its rapid, fiery train across the heavens. It flames only for a time, and soon passes away, leaving the heavens in greater darkness than before.

Love for wealth

Neither is wealth a true basis for the marriage choice. "The love of money is the root of all evil" and when it is the primary desire in marriage it acts like a canker-worm upon domestic peace and happiness. With too many in this day of money-making, marriage is but a financial speculation, a mere gold and silver affair; and their match-making is but money-making, that is, money makes the match. Many parents (but we don't call such Christians,) sacrifice their children upon the altar of mammon, and prostitute their earthly and eternal happiness to their love of filthy lucre.

Fatal mistake! Will money make your children happy? Is it for money you have them led to the bridal altar? Ah! That sordid dust may cover the grave of their fondest hopes and connubial felicity. Wed not your children to mere dollars and cents. The hand that holds a purse and shakes it before you for your child, may hold also a dagger for both the child and the parent. Look not only for riches, lest "thou be mated with misery." Wealth is good in its place, and we should not object to it, other things being equal. But it never was nor can be good as an inducement to marry. What a miserable policy it is, to make it the test of a proper match! Do not make the metals of earth the cord of the marriage tie. They are too brittle in their nature to do so. They take to themselves wings and fly away. The fine gold becomes dim and their cords are like ropes of glass-sand,

"Like the spider's most attenuated thread, they break at every breeze."

Love for rank

Rank also is a false standard of judgment in the forming of a marriage alliance. Many look only to positional society, make it everything, and think that acknowledged social distinction will compensate for the want of all other interests. While there should be a social adaptation of character, and while you should-

"Be joined to your equal in rank, or the foot of pride will kick at you,"

Yet there is nothing to justify marrying a person because of his or her social position. The evils of this may be seen in the first classes of English society, here rank is mechanical and where law forbids a trespass upon it's bastard prerogatives; and as a consequence, relatives intermarry until their descendants have degenerated into complete physical and mental imbecility. Such nepotism as this is replete with untold disaster both in the family and in the state. Too many in our democratic country copy this, look to rank, and are blind to all things else. The fruits of this are seen in that codfish aristocracy which floats with self-inflated importance upon the troubled waters of society, causing too many of the little fish to float after them, until they land themselves in the deep and muddy waters of domestic ruin.

Chapter Four

True Tests

True tests in the selection of a companion for life

Having considered some of the false standards of judgment in the choice of a companion for life, we now revert to those true tests which are given us in the word of God. There we have the institution and true idea of marriage, and the principles upon which we should proceed in making the marriage choice.

Marriage is a divine relationship

We are taught in the Holy Scriptures, the primary importance of judicious views of the nature and responsibilities of the marriage institution itself. We should apprehend it, not from its mere worldly standpoint, not as a simple legal alliance, not only as a scheme for temporal welfare and happiness, but as a divine institute, a religious alliance, involving moral responsibilities, and momentous consequences for eternity as well as for time, for soul as well as for body. We are commanded to look to its religious elements and duties; and to regard it with that solemnity of feeling which it truly demands. When the light of the bridal day throws upon the cheek its brightest colors, even then we should rejoice with trembling, and our joy and festivity should be only in the Lord.

"Joy, serious and sublime, such as doth nerve the energies of prayer, should swell the bosom, when a maiden's hand, filled with life's dewy flowerets, girds on that harness which the ministry of death alone unloose, but whose fearful power may stamp the sentence of eternity."

In the days of our forefathers, marriage was thus held sacred, as a divine institution, involving moral and religious duties and responsibilities; and their celebration of it was, therefore, a religious one. They realized its momentous import, and its bearing upon their future welfare. It was not, therefore, without heavings of deep moral emotion and the flow of tears as well as of joyful spirits, that they put the wedding garment on.

"There are smiles and tears in that gathering band, where the heart is pledged with the trembling hand. What trying thoughts in the bosom swell, as the bride bids parents and home farewell! Kneel down by the side of the tearful fair, and strengthen the perilous hour with prayer!"

True reciprocal affection

True love in each, and reciprocated by each, must determine the marriage choice. The marriage of children should not be forced. Mutual love is the basis of a proper union, because marriage is a voluntary compact. When parents, therefore, force their children into an alliance, they usurp their undoubted natural and religious rights. Hence there should be no must, where there is no will, on the part of the child. That choice which is made upon any other than reciprocated affection, is an unreasonable and irreligious one. "Parents have no right," says Paley, "to urge their children upon a marriage to which they are averse;" "add to this," says he, "that compulsion in marriage necessarily leads to prevarication; as the reluctant party promises an affection, which neither exists, nor is expected to take place." To proceed to marriage, therefore in face of absolute dislike and revulsion, is irrational and sinful.

True mutual love

As true, mutual love is the basis of marriage, so also should it be a standard of our judgment in the marriage choice. Without it, neither beauty, wealth nor rank will make home happy. True love should be such as is upheld in scripture. It is above mere passion. It never fails. It is life-like and never dies out. It is an evergreen in the bosom of home. It has moral stamina, is regulated by moral law, has a moral end, contains moral principle, and rises superior to mere prudential considerations. It is more than mere feeling or emotion; it is not blind, but rational, and above deception, having its ground in our moral and religious nature. It extends to the whole person, to body, mind, and spirit, to the character as well as to the face and form. It is tempered with respect, yea, vitalized, purified, directed and elevated by true piety. Such love alone will survive the charms and allurements of novelty, the fascinations of sense, the ravages of disease and time, and will receive sanction of heaven.

Compatible social character

Mutual adaption of character and position is another scripture standard of judgment. Is that person suited for me? Will that character make my home happy? Could I be happy with such a one? Are we congenial in spirit, sentiment, principle, cultivation, education, morals and religion? Can we sympathize and work harmoniously together in mind and heart and will and taste? Do we complement each other? These are questions of far greater importance than the question of wealth, of beauty, or of rank.

Similarity of circumstances

Fitness of circumstances, means, and age should be also considered. Am I able to support a family? Can I discharge the duties of a household? Where there is ignorance of household duties, indolence, the want of any visible means of supporting a family, no trade, no education, no energy, and no prospects, there is no reason to think there can be a proper marriage. Thus, then mutual love, adaptation of character, of means, of circumstances, of position, and of age, should be considered, in the formation of a marriage alliance.

Compatible spiritual character

But the standard of judgment to which the scriptures especially direct our attention is, that of religious equality, or spiritual adaptation. "Be not unequally yoked together with unbelievers."The positive command here is, that Christians should marry only in the Lord. Here is a test in the selection of a companion for life, from which neither parents nor children should ever depart. It forbids a matrimonial union with those who have no sympathy with religion. We should make more account of religious equality than of equality of rank and wealth. Is not true piety of more importance than education, affluence or social distinction?

Enjoyment will be impossible when unequally yoked

When husband and wife are unequally yoked together in soul and grace, their home must suffer spiritually as well as temporally. The performance of religious duties and the enjoyment of religious privileges, will be impossible. The unbeliever will discourage, oppose, and often ridicule, the pious efforts of the believer. Partiality will be produced, and godliness will decline, for, says Peter, "Unless we dwell as heirs together of the grace of life, our prayers will be hindered." The pious one cannot rule in such a home. Thus divided and striving with each other, their house must fall. Where one draws heavenward and the other hellward, opposite attractions will be presented, and the believer will find constant obstructions to growth in grace, to the discharge of parental duty, and to the cultivation of Christian graces in the heart. How can the unbeliever return, like David, to bless his household? How can he bring up his children in the nurture and admonition of the Lord? Can he be the head of a Christian home? And, tell me, does the true Christian desire any other than a Christian home? "How can two walk together, except they be agreed?" And are you, then, in your marriage, agreed to walk with the unbeliever in the broad road of sin and death? You are not if you are a true Christian!

Unequal yoking prohibited

We see, therefore, the importance of a rigid adherence to the scripture standard, "Be not unequally yoked together with unbelievers." It is even desirable that husband and wife belong to the same branch of the church, that they may walk together on the Sabbath to the house of God. There is indeed something repugnant to the feelings of a Christian to see the husband go in one direction to worship, and the wife in another. They cannot be thus divided without serious injury to the religious interests of their family, as well as of their own souls. It is impossible for them to train up their children successfully when they are separated by denominational differences. It is a matter of very common observation that when persons thus divided marry, the one or the other suffers in religious interest. From these and other considerations, we think it expedient to marry, if possible, within the pales of our own branch of the church. Then, being agreed, they can walk together with one mind and one purpose.

The peril of walking with one on the broad road

But how much more important that they be united in their pilgrim walk to eternity, united in the Lord Jesus Christ, by a common life and faith and hope! We believe that Christians commit a sin when they violate this law of religious equality, and unite themselves in matrimony with those who pay no regard to religion. Who can estimate the peril of that home in which one of its members is walking in the narrow way to heaven, while the other one is traveling in the broad road to perdition! Whom, think you, will the children follow? Let the sad experience of a thousand homes respond. Let the blighted hopes and the unrequited affections of the pious wife, reply. Let those children whose infamy and wretchedness have broken the devout mother's heart, or brought the gray hairs of the pious father down with sorrow to the grave, speak forth the answer. It will show the importance of the scripture rule before us, and will declare the sin of violating that rule.

The miseries of unequal yoking

And does not, therefore, a terrible judgment accompany that indiscriminate matrimonial union with the unbelieving world, of which so many Christians, in the present day, are guilty? Parents encourage their pious children to marry unbelievers, though they are well aware that such unholy mixtures are expressly forbidden, and that spiritual harmony is essential to their happiness. "She is at liberty to be married to whom she will, only in the Lord!" Those who violate this cardinal law of marriage, must expect to suffer the penalties attached to it. History is the record of this. The disappointed hopes, and the miseries of unnumbered homes speak forth their execution. This great scripture law has its foundation in the very nature of marriage itself. If marriage involves the law of spiritual harmony; if, in the language of the Roman law, it is "the union of a man and woman, constituting an united habitual course of life, never to be separated;" if it is a partnership of the whole life, a mutual sharing in all rights, human and divine; if they are one flesh, one in all the elements of their moral being, as Christ and His church are one; if it is a mystery of man's being, antecedent to all human law; if, in a word, man and woman in marriage, are no more two, but one flesh; and if the oneness of our nature is framed of the body, the soul, and the spirit, then is it not plain that when two persons marry, who possess no spiritual fitness for, or harmony with, each other, they violate the fundamental law of wedlock; and their marriage cannot meet the scripture conception of matrimonial union or oneness. There will be no adaptation of the whole nature for each other; they will not appreciate the sacred mysteriousness of marriage; instead of the moral and religious development of the spiritual nature, there will be the evolution of selfishness and sensuality as the leading motives of domestic life, we see, then, that the Christian cannot with impunity, violate the scripture law, "Be not unequally yoked with unbelievers."

Disregarding the prohibition of God

Shall the Christian parent and child disregard this prohibition of God? Will you ridicule this fundamental principle of Christian marriage? Will the children of God not hesitate to marry the children of the devil? Can these walk together in domestic union and harmony? Can saint and sinner be of one mind, one spirit, one life, one hope, one interest? Can the children of the light and the children of darkness, opposite in character and in their apprehension of things, become flesh of each other's flesh, and by the force of their blended light and darkness shed around their fireside the cheerfulness of a mutual love, of a common life and hope, and of a progressive spiritual work?

The duty of parents to interfere when this law is violated

Parents! It is your right and duty to interfere when your children violate this law. Bring them up from infancy to respect it. In the parlor, train them to appreciate its religious importance, show them that God will visit the iniquity of their departure from it, unto the third and fourth generation. You are stimulated to do so by the divine promise that when they grow old, they will not depart from it.

Such unequal matches are not made in heaven. God's hand is not over such matches. "What fellowship hath light with darkness?" If love, in Christian marriages, is holy and includes the religious element, then it is evident that the Christian alliance with one between whom and himself there is no religious affinity whatever, is not only an outrage against the marriage institution, but also exposes his home to the curse of God, making it a Babel of confusion and of moral antipathies.

Scriptural examples

Both the old and the new testaments give explicit testimony to the law of spiritual harmony in marriage. Thus the law of Moses forbade the children of Israel to intermarry among heathen nations. "Neither shalt thou make marriages with them; your daughter thou shalt not give unto his son, nor his daughter shalt thou take unto your son." Deut. 7:3 Abraham obeyed this law in the part he took in the marriage of his son Isaac, as recorded in the twenty-fourth chapter of Genesis. His obedience was reproduced in Isaac and Rebecca, who manifested the same desire, and took the same care that Jacob should take a wife from among the covenant people of God. See twenty-eighth chapter of Genesis.

Consequences of violating this principle

The evil consequences of the violation of this law may be seen in the history of Solomon, I. Kings, chap. 11; also in the case mentioned in the 10th chap.; and in Nehemiah, chap. 13. Paul upholds this law when he exhorts the Corinthians to marry "only in the Lord." Reason itself advocates this law. The true Christian labors for heaven and walks in the path of the just; the unbelieving labor for earth, mind only the things of this world, and walk in the broad road to ruin. Can these now walk together, live in harmony, when so widely different in spirit, in their aims and pursuits? "What fellowship hath righteousness with unrighteousness? What part hath he that believes with an infidel? And what agreement hath the temple of God with idols? For ye are the temple of the living God; as God hath said, I will dwell in them; and I will be their God, and they shall be my people. Wherefore come out from among them, and be ye separate, saith the Lord, and touch not the unclean thing; and I will receive you, and will be a father unto you, and ye shall be my sons and daughters."

It neutralizes family and church

The primitive Christians developed this law in their families. They forbade marriage with Jews, Pagans, Mohammedans, and ungodly persons. With them, piety was the first consideration in marriage. The sense of the Christian Church has ever been against religious inequity in marriage. It has always been felt to be detrimental to personal piety and to the general interests of Christianity. It limits and neutralizes the influence of the church and brings overwhelming temptations to luke-warmness in family re ligion, and is, in a word, in almost every instance, the fruitful cause of spiritual declension wherever it is practiced.

Let me, then, exhort you to marry only in the Lord. Such a union will be blessed. Daughter of Zion! marry such a man as will, like David, return to bless his household. Son of the Christian home! marry no woman who has not in her heart the casket of piety. Make this your standard; and your home shall be a happy, as well as a holy home, and

"In the blissful vision, each shall share as much of glory as his soul can bear !"

Chapter Five

Inheritance

Providing a superior inheritance

"Give me enough, saith wisdom; for he fears to ask for more; and that, by the sweat of my brow, adds stout-hearted independence; give me enough, and not less, for want is leagued with the tempter; poverty shall make a man desperate, and hurry him ruthless into crime; give me enough, and not more, saving for the children of distress; wealth oftentimes kills, where want but hinders the budding."

The children's inheritance is a vital subject. It involves the great question, "What should Christian parents leave to their children as a true inheritance from the Christian home?" We shall return but a very brief and general answer.

The idea of the home-inheritance is generally confined to the amount of wealth which descends from the parent to the child. And this is indeed too often the only inheritance of which children can boast. Many parents, who even claim to be Christians, enslave both themselves and their families to secure for their offspring a large pecuniary, inheritance. They prostitute every thing else to this. And hence it often happens that the greatest money-inheritance becomes the children's greatest curse, running them into all the wild and immoral excesses of prodigality; and ending in abject poverty, licentiousness, and disgrace; or perhaps making them like their deluded parent, penurious, covetous, and contracted in all their views and sentiments.

More than gold and silver

We think, therefore, that the children's inheritance should be more than gold and silver. This may pamper the body: but will afford no food for the mind and spirit. We do not mean by these remarks, that their inheritance should not include wealth. On the other hand, we believe that parents should make pecuniary provision for them, that they may not begin life totally destitute. But we mean, that when this is the only inheritance they receive, it often proves a curse, because it tends to destroy their sympathy with higher interests, exposes them to the uncertainties of wealth, and makes them dependent upon that alone. If it should elude their grasp, all is gone, and they become poor and helpless indeed.

What, therefore, besides wealth, should be the children's inheritance from the Christian home? We briefly answer.

Marks of a good inheritance

1. A good character. This is more valuable than wealth; for a good name is rather to be chosen than great riches. This character should be physical, intellectual, and moral. Give your children the boon of good health by a proper training to exercise and industry. Transmit to them the inheritance of good physical habits by educating their bodies, and developing their material existence according to the principles of natural law. Develop their intellectual faculties, and enrich them with the treasures of knowledge. Give character to their minds as well as to their bodies, and they will be blessed with an intellectual dowry which cannot be taken from them, and which will bring them an adequate recompense. Give to your children the inheritance of good and just principles. Train the heart to good morals; fill it with the treasures of virtue, of truth, of justice and of honor. Give it moral stamina. Educate the moral sense of your children. Direct the unfolding powers of their conscience; in a word, develop their moral faculties, and supply them with appropriate nutriment; mould their will; cultivate their emotions; rule their desires and passions; and thus unfold their moral nature according to the rules of God's revealed law.

Such a character, involving a true and vigorous evolution of body, mind and spirit, is an effectual safeguard against the evils of prodigality, the disgrace of penuriousness, and the woes of vice and crime. Their property may burn down, and they may be robbed of their gold; but neither the flame nor the robber can deprive them of their character; their intellectual and moral worth is beyond the power of man to destroy; no enemy can rob them of those virtues which a well-developed mind and heart afford; they will be to them a standing capital to enrich them in all that is essential to human happiness.

2. A good occupation is another inheritance which should descend to the children of a Christian home. Bring up your children to some useful employment by which they may be able to make a comfortable living; and you thereby give them hundreds, and, perhaps, thousands of dollars per year; you give them a boon which cannot be taken from them. Many parents, hoping to secure for their children a large pecuniary inheritance, will not permit them to learn either a trade or a profession; but let them grow up in indolence and ignorance, unable as well as unwilling, to be useful either to themselves or to others, living for no purpose, and unfit even to take care of what they leave. And when their wealth descends to them, they soon spend it all in a life of dissipation; so that in a few years they find themselves poor, and friendless, and ignorant of all means of a livelihood, without character, without home, without hope, a nuisance to society, a disgrace to their parents, a curse to themselves!

3. True religion is another inheritance which should descend to the children of the Christian home. This is an undefiled and imperishable treasure, which does not become worthless at the grave, but which will continue to increase in preciousness as long as the ages of eternity shall roll on. If through the parent's pious agency, the child comes into possession of this invaluable blessing, there is given to him more than earthly treasure, more than pecuniary competency, more than a good name, or a fair reputation, or a high social position in this life;

he receives a title to and personal meetness for, the undefiled and imperishable inheritance of heaven, composed of glittering crowns of glory, of unspeakable joys, and sweet communion with all the loved and cherished there.

The superiority of a spiritual inheritance

Thus the fruits of a parent's labor for the salvation of his children constitute an infinitely more valuable inheritance than all the accumulated fruits of his industry in behalf of wealth. All the wealth, and rank, and reputation which may descend from parent to child cannot supersede the necessity of a spiritual inheritance. It is only when you minister to the spiritual wants of your children and tinge all their thoughts and feelings with a sense of eternity; when your home is made a spiritual nursery; and you work for their eternal benefit, and thereby secure for them the fulfillment of those blessed promises which God has given concerning the children of believing parents, that you leave them an inheritance worthy of the Christian home. Such a spiritual inheritance is within the power of all Christian parents to bestow. And without its enjoyment by your children, you fail to minister unto them as a faithful steward of God. You may minister to their bodies and minds; you may amass for them a fortune; you may give them an education; you may establish them in the most lucrative business; you may fit them for an honorable and responsible position; you may leave them the heritage of social and political influence; and you may caress them with all the passionate fondness of the parental heart and hand; yet, without the heritage of true piety, of the true piety of the parent reproduced in the heart and character of the child, all will be worse than vain, yea, a curse to both the parent and the children.